ASCENDANCE OF A BOOKWORM
I'll do anything to become a librarian!

Part 1 If there aren't any books, I'll just have to make some!

Volume 2

Author: **Miya Kazuki** / Artist: **Suzuka**
Character Designer: **You Shiina**

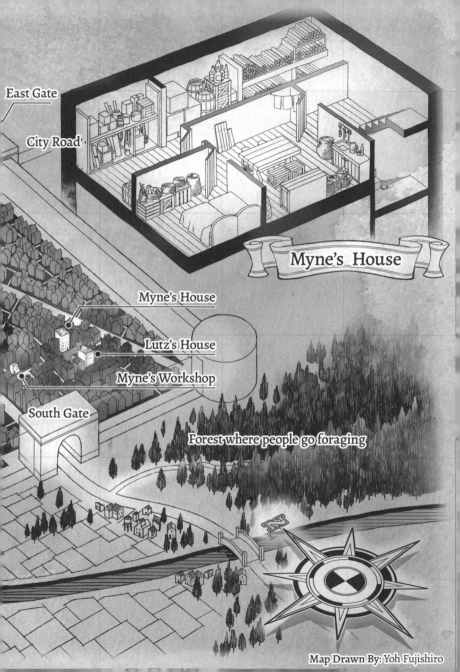

East Gate

City Road

Myne's House

Myne's House

Lutz's House

Myne's Workshop

South Gate

Forest where people go foraging

Map Drawn By: Yoh Fujishiro

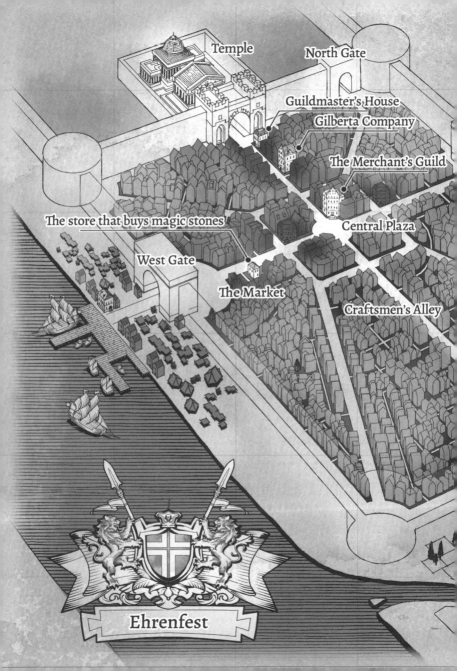

Temple

North Gate

Guildmaster's House

Gilberta Company

The Merchant's Guild

The store that buys magic stones

Central Plaza

West Gate

The Market

Craftsmen's Alley

Ehrenfest

ASCENDANCE OF A BOOKWORM
I'll do anything to become a librarian!

Part 1 If there aren't any books, I'll just have to make some!
Volume II

THIS IS A BIT SUDDEN, I KNOW.

ガラ
(Clatter)
ガラ
(Clatter)

BUT AS YOU CAN SEE,

I AM RIDING ATOP A CART.

ガラ
(Clatter)

ガラ
(Clatter)

Ch.6 Pig Killing Day

WHERE ARE WE GOING?

HEY, MOM.

TO A LITTLE FARMING TOWN NEAR THE CITY.

WE'RE BORROWING A SHED THERE.

WE'RE SMOKING MEAT?

THERE AREN'T ANY SMOKING SHEDS IN THE CITY, REMEMBER?

WHAT IN THE WORLD ARE YOU SAYING, MYNE? THIS IS COMPLETELY DIFFERENT.

OH, RIGHT. WE DID BUY A LOT OF MEAT AT THE MARKET BEFORE.

I THOUGHT WE BOILED AND SALTED IT ALL, THOUGH...

TODAY IS PIG KILLING DAY.

WHAT?!

WE GO THERE, KILL THE PIGS, BUTCHER THEM, AND SMOKE OR SALT THE MEAT TO MAKE ALL SORTS OF THINGS, LIKE SAUSAGE.

EVERYONE IN THE NEIGHBORHOOD CHIPS IN TO BUY PIGS AT THE FARMING VILLAGE.

PIG KILLING DAY?! WHAT?!

ガタタ (Clatter)

...PI...

P-P-P...

Be careful.

...I WISH I HAD CAUGHT ANOTHER FEVER THIS YEAR.

OH, THAT'S RIGHT.

MOM, SHE GOT A FEVER IN THE CART AND MISSED THE WHOLE THING.

HOW DOES A DAY LIKE THAT EXIST?!

GRACIOUS, MYNE, DON'T YOU REMEMBER LAST YEAR?

ガラ (Clatter)　ガラ (Clatter)

THIS PORK WILL BE THE BULK OF OUR MEAT. ALL THAT WAS JUST A LITTLE EXTRA ON TOP OF IT.

YOU KNOW THAT WON'T BE ENOUGH.

DIDN'T WE ALREADY BUY MEAT, ANYWAY?

I HAD THOUGHT ALL THAT MEAT WE BOUGHT WOULD BE ENOUGH. I WAS WRONG.

UNLIKE JAPAN, THIS WORLD DOESN'T HAVE ANY YEAR-ROUND SUPER-MARKETS.

I KNEW WE NEEDED TO PRE-PARE FOR WINTER AHEAD OF TIME, BUT...

MYNE.

THEY SURE BROUGHT IN A LOT OF FIREWOOD, TOO. ARE THE WIN-TERS SO BAD HERE YOU CAN'T EVEN GO OUTSIDE?

ふ ふ ふ
(Ahaha)

IT'S KINDA LIKE A TINY FESTIVAL FOR US NEIGHBORS!

TODAY WE'LL GET TO TASTE-TEST THE PORK WHILE IT'S BEING MADE, EAT FRESH SAUSAGE FOR SUPPER...

THERE'S LOTS OF FUN STUFF ABOUT PIG KILLING DAY!

GUUUH.

NEIGH-BORS, HUH...

I DON'T WANNA GO...

ガラ
(Clatter)

ガラ
(Clatter)

I BET THERE WILL BE A LOT OF PEOPLE I DON'T KNOW...

(Blurry)
モヤァ

A LOT OF MYNE'S MEMORIES ARE VAGUE, SO...

DON'T BE SILLY.

はぁ
(Haaah)

NOT ONLY THAT, BUT WE HAVE TO BUTCHER A PIG TODAY...

OKAY, WE'RE GOING THROUGH THE GATE.

チカ
(Shine)

9

(Caw)

(Stretch)

THIS FEELS TOTALLY DIFFERENT FROM BEING SURROUNDED BY WALLS.

THE AIR TASTES SO GOOD!

(Clatter)

(Clatter)

WOOOW.

(Clatter)

ガ (Thunk)
ガー

MYNE. YOU'LL BITE YOUR TONGUE IF YOU DON'T CLOSE YOUR MOUTH.

BWUH?!

ガタ (Clatter)
ガタ (Clatter)

AH, WAH!

AH!

ガタ (Clatter)

LEARN ABOUT ASPHALT!

(Rattle) ガラ
(Rattle) ガラ..

(Clatter) ガラ
(Clatter) ガラ

THIS ROAD'S BUMPY WHEN IT'S SUNNY...

...AND MUDDY WHEN IT'S RAINY! IT'S THE WORST!

ギ (Squeeze) ゅっ

11

わい (Chatter)

わい (Chatter)

ガ (Dash)

RIGHT!

(Fwoosh)

RUN, TUULI!

CRAP, THEY'RE ALREADY STARTING!

EFFA, TUULI! HURRY UP AND GO!

ガッ (Rustle)

Ah!

OH NO!

WHA?

(Rustle)

WELL, WATCHING OVER THE CART'S PRETTY IMPORTANT, RIGHT?

トフッ (Fwump)

MHM, SUPER IMPORTANT.

ポツ (All Alone)

......

THEY LEFT ME...

OH!

IT'S FEY.

Pink head.

I WONDER IF LUTZ IS OVER THERE TOO.

SQUEE!

HUH?

NO WAY.

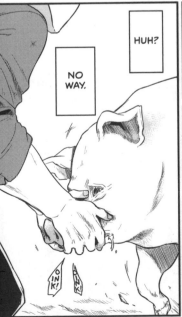

(ONK!) (ONK!)

(Shout) わあ

ONK!

(Shout) わあ

(Trot) ズズッ (Trot)

HERE I GO!

RIGHT IN FRONT OF ME?

DST

GRAH!

AB!)

NO WAY...

THAT'S JUST...

KYAAAH!

(Cheer!)

14

ズル
(Pour)
GUSH!
NGH!
UGH...
THEY'RE SO EFFICIENT IT'S SCARY.
(Stir)
(Stir)
(Creak)
ギッ
(Creak)
ギッ

(Waver)

GUH.

AH.

I THINK

I'M...

DONE.

(Slice)

(Crackle)

(Crackle)

...I GUESS I PASSED OUT AGAIN.

...IN-SIDE.

I'M INSIDE.

すりるっ
(Slip)

ドサッ!!
(Thump)

BWUH?!

...WHERE AM I?

キゅっ
(Squeeze)

OWWW...

スッ
(Sniff)

WHY'S EVERY-THING GOING WRONG TODAY...?

17

HEYA!

MR. OTTO?

Oh!

FINALLY AWAKE, HUH?

THIS MUST BE A WAITING ROOM IN THE GATE, THEN.

HAHA.

OF COURSE I DO!

TAP. TAP.

YOU REMEMBER ME, THEN?

THAT'S A RE-LIEF.

Whew

HE SAID YOU PASSED OUT IN THE CART.

THE CAPTAIN CAME RUSHING BACK WITH YOU IN HIS ARMS, LOOKING HORRIFIED.

HE TOLD ME HE'D BE BACK AS SOON HE FINISHES WHAT HE HAS TO DO.

うぷ
(Mph)

I FEEL GROSS JUST REMEMBERING IT... I'M GONNA HAVE NIGHTMARES ABOUT THIS.

AAAH.

WHAT'S WRONG, MYNE?

FEELING LONELY WITHOUT YOUR MOM AND DAD?

ポス
(Fwump)

...BUTCHERING A PIG AND PREPARING ALL THE MEAT WILL PROBABLY TAKE A LONG TIME, HUH?

19

RIGHT.

ANYWAY, GOOD TIMING.

NUH UH. I WAS JUST WONDER-ING HOW I SHOULD KILL TIME.

...OH YEAH. THEY DID SAY YOU WERE MORE MATURE THAN YOU LOOK.

?

THIS'LL BE GREAT FOR KILL-ING TIME, RIGHT?

I BROUGHT IT SINCE I KNEW FOR SURE YOU'D PASS BY THE GATE TODAY.

THANK YOU SO MUCH!

WOOOW! THE STONE SLATE!

つ`丶`
(Scribble)

つ`丶`
(Scribble)

MR. OTTO, YOU'RE AMAZING!

Just one second.

A MAN OF CULTURE WHO'S NICE AND CONSIDERATE?

(Scritch)

カ゛丨丨

(Scratch)

カ゛丨丨

HERE. IT'S YOUR NAME.

I NEED TO GO BACK TO WATCHING THE GATE. PRACTICE A LITTLE, OKAY?

"MYNE"

MY HEART'S BEATING SO HARD...

WOW...

カリ
(Scritch)

SCRITCH.

LET-TERS...

I'M WRITING LETTERS!

I HAD NO IDEA JUST READ-ING AND WRITING LETTERS COULD MAKE ME SO HAPPY.

...AAAH, I'M SO HAPPY.

(Grin)

カリ
(Scritch)
カリ
(Saritch)

いろはにほへ
ちりぬるを
わかよた

(Wipe) ゴ
(Wipe) こ
ゴ
こ

ゴーーン
(Dooon!)
ゴーン
(Dooon!)
ゴーーン…
(Dooon!)
DOOON

(Scritch) カリカリ
(Scratch) カリ
(Scritch) カリカリ
(Scratch) カリ

しゃいーん
(Shiiine)

THIS IS SO FUN...!

MYNE?!

DID YOU GET A FEVER?!

グラ)グラ
(Guuuuuh~)

C- Captaaaaain!

SORRY FOR THE WAIT, MYNE.

THE CAPTAIN IS BA—

I CAN'T BELIEVE I GOT SICK WITH A FURNACE RIGHT NEXT TO ME.

Haah.

I BROUGHT YOU SOUP, MYNE.

JUST GET SOME REST!

...OKAY.

STOP TRYING TO GET OUT OF BED, YOU HAVE A FEVER!

MYNE!

I MEAN... OKAY, YOU DIDN'T PROMISE THAT.

BUT ISN'T IT STILL, LIKE, AN UN-SPOKEN PROMISE?

We're not even done preparing for winter yet.

SERI-OUSLY, THIS IS A REAL PAIN.

SORRY, TUULI.

I NEVER PROM-ISED THAT!

AWW, WHAT? DIDN'T YOU PROMISE NOT TO SAY THAT?

(Munch) もぐ もぐ (Munch)

THE SOUP KINDA JUST TASTES LIKE SALT.

BUT THIS SAUSAGE SURE IS GREAT.

(Haah)

カパパ (Clatter)

NOT BAD.

I THINK GETTING TO READ A BOOK WOULD SEND ME OVER THE MOON.

...IF JUST WRITING LETTERS IS ENOUGH TO MAKE ME FEEL THIS HAPPY,

I NEED TO GET BETTER SOON SO I CAN START MAKING PAPER.

Ch.6: Pig Killing Day End

AND EVENTUALLY... TRUE WINTER FELL UPON THE CITY.

ビュオオ…
(Whoosh)

SEVERAL MONTHS PASSED SINCE I ARRIVED IN THIS WORLD.

パチ
(Crackle)

(Crackle)
パチ

...IT'S DARK.

(Crackle)
パチ

(Crackle)
パチ

Haaah...

Ch.7 The Sweet Taste of Winter

THAT'S JUST HOW IT IS DURING BLIZZARDS.

(Stitch)

(Stitch)

WHY'S IT THIS DARK AT NOON?

HEY, MOM.

IS EVERYONE'S HOME THIS DARK?

NGH...

WE NEED TO PRESERVE OIL, SO IT'S FOR EMERGENCIES ONLY.

(Snip)

LET'S USE THAT LAMP, THEN.

I'VE HEARD THAT SOMEWHAT RICH FAMILIES HAVE SEVERAL LAMPS, BUT...

WE ONLY HAVE ONE.

YOU DON'T WANT US TO RUN OUT IF WINTER DRAGS ON, DO YOU?

AW...

IT'S GO- ING TO BE THIS DARK ALL WINTER?

I'M NOT READING BOOKS OR ANYTHING, BUT THIS IS REALLY GOING TO HURT MY VISION.

Scrape

TUULI, YOUR BAPTISM IS COMING UP, SO I THINK IT'S ABOUT TIME FOR YOU TO LEARN SOME WORKING SKILLS.

FIRST YOU PREPARE THE WARP.

TAKE THE THREAD AND...

OH, RIGHT. TUULI WANTS TO BECOME A SEAM- STRESS, I THINK.

She's a hard worker.

COME WITH ME, DEAR.

I'LL TEACH YOU HOW TO WEAVE CLOTH.

OKAAAY.

IF I WEAVE THESE PLANT FIBERS TOGETHER, IT SHOULD DEFINITELY TURN INTO SOMETHING LIKE PAPER.

ドサッ

(Rustle)

FIGHT!

I WON'T LOSE TO ANCIENT EGYPTIANS!

(Ding)

(Fiddle)
ちま…

I JUST NEED TO LINE THE FIBERS UP VERTICALLY, THEN WEAVE THE OTHERS IN HORIZONTALLY...

ちま…
(Fiddle)

キリ (Push)
ゆっ

32

MYNE, IF YOU HAVE TIME TO PLAY AROUND, MAKE BASKETS INSTEAD.

GUH. THE FIBERS ARE SO SMALL MY EYES ARE HURTING.

(Fiddle) ちま

ちま (Fiddle)

MMM.

MAYBE WHEN I'M DONE.

カッ (Swoosh)

カッ (Swoosh)

NGH... FIX IT, FIX IT...

AH! I MESSED UP!

HMM?

[FAUX-PAPYRUS].

HEY, WHAT ARE YOU MAKING, ANYWAY?

GEEZ!

AHHH, NOT AGAIN!

MYNE... IT'S NOT GETTING MUCH BIGGER.

I KNOW THAT!

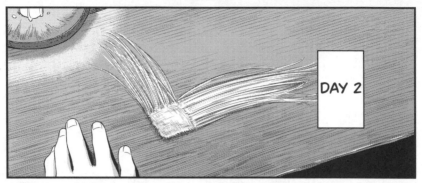

DAY 2

DAY 3

.....

MYNE...

HEY, MYNE.

YOU'VE BEEN MAKING THAT FOR DAYS AND I STILL DON'T GET WHAT IT IS.

MYNE?

Haah...

うガ (GYAAAAH!)

YOU WIN, ANCIENT EGYPTIANS!

THAT'S IT!

I CAN'T TAKE THIS ANY-MORE!

ヒクヒク (Jolt)

BE QUIET, MYNE.

STOP PLAYING AROUND WITH GRASS AND WEAVE BASKETS!

MY PAPYRUS PLAN...

うう゛゛゛... (Waaaaah...)

WHO KNOWS HOW MANY DAYS IT'LL TAKE JUST TO MAKE A POSTCARD'S WORTH OF PAPER.

FIDDLE, FIDDLE, FIDDLE, DAY IN, DAY OUT...

NGH...

I DON'T KNOW WHAT YOU'RE TALKING ABOUT, BUT YOU FAILED TO MAKE WHATEVER YOU WERE TRYING TO, RIGHT?

.....

BASKETS AREN'T BOOKS...

I'LL GIVE UP ON FAUX-PAPYRUS.

...OKAAAY.

IT'S TOO MUCH FOR ME TO MAKE ALONE...

JUST MAKE BASKETS ALREADY.

WANT ME TO TEACH YOU HOW TO MAKE THEM?

UH HUH.

TUULI.

I'LL MAKE SOME BASKETS TOO. CAN I HAVE SOME WOOD?

ぐいっ (Push) ぐいっ (Push)

NO, THAT'S OKAY. I KNOW HOW ALREADY.

WHA?

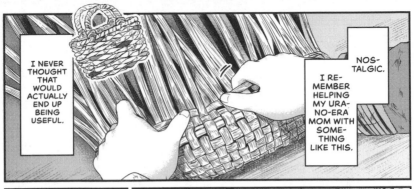

I NEVER THOUGHT THAT WOULD ACTUALLY END UP BEING USEFUL.

NOSTALGIC. I REMEMBER HELPING MY URA-NO-ERA MOM WITH SOMETHING LIKE THIS.

.....

WE ROLLED NEWSPAPER INTO THIN STRIPS TO MAKE BASKETS.

THAT THREAD LOOKS REALLY THIN.

IS THAT FOR TUULI'S SPECIAL DRESS?

IT IS.

カタン
(Clack)

カタン
(Clack)

WHY ARE YOU MAKING SUMMER CLOTHES IN THE WINTER?

WON'T TUULI GET BIGGER BY THEN?

シュルル
(Swoosh)

TUULI'S BAPTISM IS IN THE SUMMER, AFTER ALL.

I'M MAINLY WORRIED ABOUT HOW IT WILL BE TOO BIG FOR YOU TO WEAR AS A HAND-ME-DOWN, MYNE.

I CAN ADJUST IT A LIT-TLE, SO THAT'S NOT A PROB-LEM.

だ ぼっ
(Flop)

THICK THREAD WOULD JUST BE TOO HOT.

BUT WHY?

Wha?

BEAUTY?

YOU NEED TO START LEARN-ING HOW TO WEAVE TOO, MYNE.

YOU CAN'T BE A BEAUTY IF YOU DON'T KNOW HOW TO SEW AND WEAVE.

WHAT SHOULD I DO NEXT YEAR, I WONDER?

HMM...

SOUNDS SERIOUS.

38

...AHH. MAYBE I'D BE INTERESTED IN IT IF I COULD WEAVE THREAD INTO PAPER.

...AHH. I'M DEFINITELY NOT GOING TO BE A BEAUTY, THEN.

MAKING YOUR FAMILY'S CLOTHES IS IMPORTANT BOTH FOR PRIDE AND PRACTICALITY, ISN'T IT?

THAT'S WHY YOU HAVE TO BE GOOD AT SEWING AND COOKING TO BE A BEAUTY.

I THINK YOU WOULD DO REALLY WELL AS AN APPRENTICE CARPENTER!

AMAZING, MYNE!

THAT'S A BIT...

...WHEW. ALL DONE.

I MADE HER SAD?!

しゅん。 (Depressed)

I'M SUPPOSED TO BE THE OLDER SISTER...

ぐ (Ngh...)

...WHY ARE YOU SO GOOD AT THIS, MYNE?

39

YOU'RE BETTER THAN ME AT OTHER THINGS SINCE YOU DIDN'T JUST STAY HOLED UP INSIDE MAKING BASKETS, RIGHT?

I'VE BEEN MAKING BASKETS ALL THE TIME WHILE YOU'VE BEEN AT THE FOREST, SO IT MAKES SENSE THAT I'M BETTER!

UMMM... OH YEAH!

MRS. GERDA TAUGHT ME HOW TO MAKE THESE WHILE SHE WAS BABY-SITTING!

...HUH, OKAY.

LIKE, I'M HONESTLY JEALOUS OF HOW MUCH BETTER YOU ARE THAN ME AT EVERY-THING ELSE!

わた (Panic)

Umm, uhh...

SO DON'T WORRY ABOUT IT!

わた (Panic)

ほっ (Whew)

UH HUH!

YOU'LL GET BET-TER THAN ME IN NO TIME, TUULI.

THEN I'LL JUST HAVE TO MAKE LOTS OF BASKETS THIS WINTER AND GET BETTER THAN YOU, MYNE.

MESO-POTAMIAN CULTURE, OF COURSE!

EGYPTIAN CULTURE WASN'T IT... SO WHAT'S NEXT?

...BEING GOOD AT MAKING BASKETS DOESN'T MAKE ME FEEL ANY BETTER.

ALL I WANT IS BOOKS.

LONG LIVE MESO-POTAMIAN CULTURE!

...I REMEMBER CUNEIFORM.

I REMEMBER CLAY TABLETS!

OKAY, THAT'S THE NEW PLAN!

I'LL MAKE CLAY TABLETS AND CARVE LETTERS INTO THEM.

EVEN A CHILD SHOULD BE ABLE TO HEAT UP TABLETS IN A FURNACE.

I'LL MAKE CLAY TABLETS ONCE THE SNOW MELTS AND SPRING COMES!

DON'T BE SILLY, MYNE.

IS IT SPRING?

(Snuggle) もぞ

...NMM?

(Slam) ハブーノッ

DAD, IT'S SUNNY OUTSIDE!

IT'S SUNNY!

(Push) ぐいい

(Push) ぐいい

COME ON, WAKEY WAKEY.

I'M GONNA HIBERNATE, WAKE ME WHEN IT'S SPRING...

GUUUH, SO COLD...

すぅ
(Zzz)

DON'T EVEN THINK ABOUT IT!

LOOK AT HOW NICE THE WEATHER IS!

(Bam!)
バン

YOU NEED TO WAKE UP TOO, MYNE. EAT YOUR BREAKFAST.

ぐいーー
(Ruffle)

WE GOTTA HURRY!

YEAH, YEAH...

ポ
(Rub)
ポ
(Rub)

COME ON, DAD, DON'T YOU HAVE TODAY OFF?

...WHAT'S A "PARUE"?

BYE BYE.

WE'LL COME BACK WITH LOTS OF PARUES!

OKAY, BYE BYE!

IF YOU'RE AWAKE, EAT BREAKFAST!

MYNE!

...FIINE.

WELL, WHATEVER. BACK TO SLEEP...

WE'RE HOME!

ガチャ (Click)

THAT'S WONDERFUL, DEAR.

Phew!

I'VE ALREADY SET UP THE DISHES FOR YOU.

WE FOUND THREE WHOLE PARUES!

LIKE THIS ONE?

UH HUH, THANKS!

THAT'S A PARUE?

IT'S PURE WHITE.

MYNE, WOULD YOU GRAB A STICK FOR ME?

(Crackle) (Crackle)

(Pour) (Pour)

SQUISH.

(Drip)

HOLD DOWN THE BOWL FOR ME.

OKAY.

PARUES ARE AMAZING.

THEIR JUICE IS SWEET AND TASTY, PLUS YOU CAN SQUEEZE OIL OUT OF THEM.

ふわっ (Fwaah!)

WOW!

IT SMELLS SO SWEET!

MYNE,

YOU'VE NEVER BEEN, SO YOU DON'T KNOW THIS, BUT...

GATHERING PARUES IS REALLY HARD.

WOW, I BET PEOPLE FIGHT REALLY HARD OVER THEM.

EVEN THE LEFTOVER STUFF IS USED TO FEED ANIMALS.

YOU CAN ONLY FIND THEM ON SUNNY DAYS IN THE WINTER, SO EVERYONE HEADS TO THE FOREST SUPER EARLY IN THE MORNING.

(Pat) ポ

(Pat) ポ

THEY DO.

46

BUT YOU CAN'T EVER USE FIRE ON TOP OF A PARUE TREE.

THE TREE WILL USE ITS MYSTERIOUS POWER TO PUT OUT THE FIRE.

じゅっ (Squish)

TO GET THE FRUIT, YOU HAVE TO USE YOUR HANDS TO WARM UP THE BRANCH IT'S GROWING ON AND SOFTEN IT.

YOU'D CATCH A COLD IN SECONDS, MYNE.

BARE HANDS, IN THE WINTER?!

SO THE ONLY THING YOU CAN DO IS TAKE OFF YOUR GLOVES AND WARM IT WITH YOUR BARE HANDS.

MYSTERIOUS POWER...?

CAN'T YOU WAIT UNTIL NOON TO GET THEM, WHEN IT'S WARMER?

?

THERE'S A TIME LIMIT?

UH HUH.

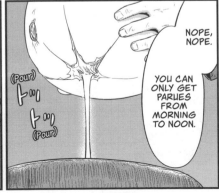

NOPE, NOPE.

YOU CAN ONLY GET PARUES FROM MORNING TO NOON.

(Pour) トッ

トッ (Pour)

THEY SHAKE THEIR BRANCHES LIKE A GIRL SHAKING THEIR HAIR THE WHOLE TIME.

LIKE, SWISH SWOOSH.

ONCE THE LEAVES START MAKING NOISE, THE PARUE TREES START GROWING REALLY TALL.

GROW-ING? SWISH SWOOSH?

THEN THEIR LEAVES START MAKING ALL SORTS OF SWISHY SWASHY NOISES.

THEY START SHINING AND SHAK-ING ALL ON THEIR OWN...

SO, LIKE, WHEN NOON COMES AND THE SUN STARTS SHINING ON THE TREES...

SHINING? SWISHY SWASHY?

(Squish)

NOPE. I CAN'T IMAGINE THAT AT ALL.

SOUNDS LIKE A WEIRD TREE...

.....

?

ピューーン

(Whoosh)

AND LASTLY, ALL THE PARUES THAT DIDN'T GET HARVESTED SHOOT AWAY!

THE TREES JUST MELT AWAY AFTER THAT.

GLUG

GLUG

YOU CAN DRINK A LITTLE ONCE I MOVE IT TO THE VASE.

OKAY, DONE.

(Gulp)

HERE.

THIS IS WHAT HAPPINESS TASTES LIKE!

!

NGH!

OKAAAY.

WE TREASURE THIS STUFF OVER THE WINTER, SO DON'T DRINK IT ALL AT ONCE.

Let me have some too!

(sp) (sp)

IT'S LIKE THICK COCONUT MILK!

DAD, ARE THESE THE LEFTOVERS?

AND IT SMELLS GOOD, TOO. WHY CAN'T WE EAT IT, AGAIN?

(Sniff)
(Sniff)

IT LOOKS LIKE OKARA*.

(Fwip)
じり

YEP.

TAKE'M TO LUTZ'S PLACE AND TRADE'M FOR EGGS, WOULD YA?

MYNE! THAT'S BIRD FOOD!

(Nom)
(Nom)
ガに
ガに
(Nom)
がに

ばん
(Stop!)

ひ
よ
い
(Plop)

(Chew)
ぱく

?!

*OKARA: SOY PULP THAT IS LEFT OVER FROM THE PRODUCTION OF SOY MILK AND TOFU.

50

WHA?

WE CAN EAT THIS STUFF.

(Gulp)

...MHM.

MYNE.

TUULI.

(Creak)

(Knock)

WE WANT TO TRADE FOR EGGS, PLEASE!

(Knock)

GOT ANY MEAT INSTEAD?

MY BROTHERS KEEP STEALING ALL OF MINE, SO I'M STARVING.

WE'VE GOT PLENTY OF BIRD FOOD ALREADY.

51

BUT IT'S GOOD.

WHO WOULD EAT BIRD FOOD?!

WHY DON'T YOU JUST EAT THIS, THEN?

HUH?!

WHAT KIND OF IDIOT WOULD WORK HARD TO GET A PARUE AND THEN JUST EAT IT?!

DOING ANYTHING ELSE WOULD JUST BE WASTING IT!

YOU JUST HAVE TO MAKE IT RIGHT.

IT ONLY GETS SO DRY BECAUSE YOU DRAIN IT SO MUCH.

(Poke)

(Poke)

...UM, LUTZ.

SERIOUSLY...?!

BUT YOU SAID YOU HAVE ENOUGH BIRD FOOD, RIGHT?

WHAT'S WRONG WITH USING THE REST TO FEED PEOPLE?

DID SHE MAKE YOU EAT BIRD FOOD?!

WAIT, WHAT?

(Pout)

RUDE!

I WAS SHOCKED BY HOW GOOD IT TASTED...

I KNOW IT'S HARD TO BELIEVE, BUT THIS STUFF REALLY IS FINE TO EAT.

HERE.

YEAH, BUT...

(Step)

(Step)

SEEING IS BELIEVING. OR TASTING IS, ANYWAY.

DO YOU HAVE ANY PARUE JUICE LEFT OVER, LUTZ?

SWEET AND TASTY!

(Nom)

UH HUH.

(Chew)

(Chew)

TRY IT.

(Swish)

(Ahh!)

OPEN WIDE, LUTZ!

(Loom)

RIGHT?

GOOD?

SWEET?

(Nom)

!

...YEAH, TASTES GOOD.

HEHEH. PRETTY SWEET, ISN'T IT?

WHAT'S YOURS IS MINE!

ビッ ドア (Thump)

HAND IT OVER, LUTZ!

ガーッ… (Jolt!)

GAAAH!

ドァ (Thump)

ガッ… (Serious!)

REALLY?!

ピッ (Freeze)

...I COULD MAKE SOMETHING BETTER HERE IF YOU LEND ME YOUR KITCHEN.

ガッ… (Freeze)

BROTHERS ARE SCARY!

ギ (Punch)

ギ (Punch)

バッ (Rush)

LEAVE IT TO US!

WHAT DO WE GOTTA DO?!

バッ (Rush)

Ah.

BUT I THINK I'LL NEED YOU TO HELP ME.

I'M NOT STRONG ENOUGH TO MAKE MUCH ON MY OWN.

ZASHA AND SIEG, HEAT A METAL PAN IN THE HEARTH.

OKAY, I'LL GIVE INSTRUCTIONS. PAY CLOSE ATTENTION.

RALPH, BRING ME A BOWL, A WOODEN SPATULA, AND A LADLE.

AND LUTZ, TWO EGGS, MILK, AND BUTTER PLEASE.

じゃか
(Stir)

じゃが!
(Stir)

RALPH, MIX ALL THIS TOGETHER UNTIL IT'S ONE BIG GLOB.

(Pour)

ALRIGHT, ALRIGHT.

EVERYONE, BE SURE TO CONTRIBUTE A LITTLE OF YOUR OWN PARUE JUICE.

IT WOULDN'T BE FAIR TO USE ALL OF LUTZ'S FOR THIS.

NOW JUST WATCH ME.

FIRST, PUT ON SOME FAT...

じゅうっ
(Sizzle)

UH HUH, PERFECT.

(Bubble)
ぶ

(Bubble)
ぶ

どろ
(Glop)

ジ
(Sizzle)
ユア

THEN, ONCE IT STARTS BUBBLING LIKE THIS, FLIP IT OVER.

HAND ME THE SPATULA, PLEASE.

Hokay.

OOOH!

(Flop)

YOU SURE?

MYNE, YOU SHOULDN'T BE DOING THAT. LET ME.

UH... WHAT?

AHH, UMMM.

SIMPLE PARUE CAKES!

(Steam)

TADAAAA!

[SIMPLE OKARA PAN-CAKES]!

(Steam)

I'M GLAD YOU ALL LIKE IT.

LET'S MAKE MORE!

IS THIS FOR REAL?!

(Nom)

ガブ

SO GOOD!

Here, Tuuli.

(Nom)

ガブ

(Nom) はぐ

(Nom) はぐ

(Chomp) ガふ

(Chomp) ガふ

THEY'RE SIMPLE TO MAKE AND FILL YOU RIGHT UP, DON'T THEY?

YUP.

YOU'RE AMAZING, MYNE.

ぐ、ん、、

(Wow...)

THIS IS GOOD.

59

I'LL MAKE THE STUFF INSTEAD IF YOU TEACH ME HOW.

YEAH, COOKING IS PRETTY HARD FOR YOU.

THERE'S OTHER RECIPES I KNOW THAT CAN USE PARUE LEFTOVERS, BUT I CAN'T MAKE THEM ON MY OWN.

(Nom) も ぐ (Nom) も ぐ

THIS FOOD'S SO GOOD, YOU'RE KIND OF LIKE A GOD TO ME NOW. SO YEAH...

(Lick) ペ ろ

Ah!

REALLY?!

I'VE GOT YOUR BACK, MYNE.

Ch.7: The Sweet Taste of Winter End

IN THIS CITY THAT HIBERNATES DURING THE WINTER, GOING OUT TO GATHER PARUES ON SUNNY DAYS SEEMS TO BE A CUSTOM.

I'M GOING WITH TUULI TO GATHER PARUES TODAY.

(Slurp) ズ ズ

I'VE GOT IT.

MMM...

GUNTHER HAS WORK, SO...

BUT I JUST DON'T KNOW WHAT TO DO ABOUT YOU, MYNE.

WHY DON'T YOU WAIT AT THE GATE WITH ME, MYNE?

WHA?

Ch.8 Helping Out Otto

I'LL COME PICK YOU UP ON THE WAY BACK, MYNE, SO BE A GOOD GIRL AND WAIT UNTIL NOON.

(Rustle)

BWUH?

THAT'S A GOOD IDEA.

I LOVE IT!

SEE YOU LATER, MYNE!

(Squeeze)

LET'S GO, TUULI.

AH.

WELL, IT MIGHT BE A NICE CHANGE OF PACE.

THE ONLY THINGS I CAN DO AT HOME ARE MAKE BASKETS AND PLAY WITH MY SLATE, ANYWAY.

......

(Shut)

YEAH, I THINK SO?

YAY!

I BETTER BRING MY SLATE, THEN.

Thanks for the meal.

OH RIGHT, DAD!

IS MR. OTTO WORKING TODAY?

(Slurp)
ズズ

...MYNE.

DO YOU REALLY LIKE OTTO THAT MUCH?

(Step)
(Step)

I'M ALL READY, DAD.

LET'S GO!

♪

(Shine)

UH-HUH!

I REALLY LIKE HIM!

Decided on her own.

AFTER ALL, HE'S THE ONE WHO GAVE ME THIS SLATE AND WILL TEACH ME TO READ.

HOW COULD I NOT LIKE HIM A LOT?

I'M GOING TO HAVE HIM TEACH ME MORE LETTERS TODAY!

YOU'RE SO TALL, DAD!

WOOOW!

64

BE SURE TO HOLD ON TIGHT, ALRIGHT?

UH HUH!

...MYNE.

(Crunch) ザク

(Crunch) ザク

THIS DEFINITELY FEELS LIKE A COUNTRY SUPER IN THE NORTH.

OTTO'S ALREADY MARRIED, Y'KNOW?

WHAT EXACTLY ARE YOU TRYING TO STOP YOUR FIVE-YEAR-OLD DAUGHTER FROM DOING?!

ザク (Crunch)

HIS WIFE IS EVERY-THING TO HIM, ALRIGHT?

UMM...

SO WHAT?

(Crunch) ザク

ピタ (Freeze)

SO BASI-CALLY, MR. OTTO'S A GREAT MAN WHO TAKES GOOD CARE OF HIS WIFE?

...NO.

(MUMBLE) ボソ

I'M JUST GONNA PRETEND I DIDN'T HEAR ANY-THING!

MY ORIGINAL DAD DIED WHEN I WAS YOUNG, BUT I'M PRETTY SURE HE WASN'T THIS MUCH OF A DAUGHTER-OBSESSED NERD.

DON'T EVEN THINK I'M GONNA BE NICE AND SAY "I LIKE YOU MORE, DAD!" OR SOMETHING!

...SO ANNOY-ING!

ザッ (Crunch)

ザッ (Crunch)

ザッ (Crunch)

ザッ (Crunch)

.....

.....

66

ペコッ
(Bow)

GOOD MORNING.

OH?

IS BOWING NOT A NORMAL THING IN THIS WORLD?

ギ,,
(Creak)

コツ
(Step)

コツ
(Step)

WHOOPS, WHOOPS.

CAPTAIN... AND MYNE?

WHAT BRINGS YOU TWO HERE?

(Creak)

COMING IN...

OTTO.

LOOK AFTER HER. GOT IT?

SHE'S WAITING HERE UNTIL EFFA FINISHES HARVESTING PARUES AND COMES TO GET HER.

UHH...

(Slam!)

MYNE, WAIT BY THE FURNACE.

THE HEAT'LL HELP STAVE OFF A COLD.

BUT, ER, I HAVE THE FINANCIAL REPORTS AND—

WHA?

IT'S JUST, I REALLY LOVE THAT STONE SLATE YOU GAVE ME.

AND I COULDN'T HELP BUT GET EXCITED TO SEE YOU AGAIN TODAY.

SORRY, MR. OTTO.

(Turn)

THAT'S FINE!

I'M HAPPY TO SEE YOU AGAIN TOO, MYNE. BUT, UH...

WELL, UM...

WHY ARE YOU APOL-OGIZING ABOUT ALL THAT?

(Rustle)

I COMPLI-MENTED YOU, AND DAD GOT JEALOUS...

AHH... THAT'LL DO IT.

HERE, LEND ME THE SLATE.

THANKS, MR. OTTO!

...YEAH, I CAN TRUST YOU ON THAT, MYNE.

(Hold Up.)

IF YOU TEACH ME LETTERS, I'LL STAY QUIET AND PRACTICE.

(Scratch)
(Scratch)

...WHEW.

I THINK I'VE LEARNED A LOT.

コツ (Scratch)

コツ (Scratch)

コツ (Scratch)

70

(Clink)

(Clink)

WRITING OUT FINANCIAL REPORTS AND BUDGETS.

WE HAVE TO FINISH AND DELIVER A FULL YEAR'S BUDGET BEFORE THE WINTER IS UP.

PROBLEM IS, NOT MANY SOLDIERS ARE GOOD AT FINANCIAL STUFF.

(Whew)

MR. OTTO, WHAT ARE YOU DOING?

THAT SOUNDS LIKE A REAL PAIN.

THE RESULT? I'M GOOD WITH MONEY, SO ALL THIS WORK GETS PUSHED ONTO ME.

IS THIS ORDERING NEW EQUIPMENT AND STUFF?

OH!

IF THIS IS THE PRICE AND THIS IS THE TOTAL BEING ORDERED,

HERE. THIS IS 75 AND 30, RIGHT?

7いッ (Point)

SHOULDN'T IT MULTIPLY TO 2,250?

MR. OTTO, ISN'T THIS WRONG?

HUH?

MY MOM TAUGHT ME NUMBERS AT THE MARKET.

...I THOUGHT YOU DIDN'T KNOW HOW TO READ.

HOW CAN YOU DO MATH?

Oh.

THIS IS WRONG TOO.

SO, I CAN DO MATH, BUT I CAN'T READ THE WORDS BESIDE THE NUMBERS AT ALL.

?

.....

WOULD YOU PLEASE HELP ME?

...MYNE.

I'M GOING TO SWALLOW MY PRIDE TO ASK THIS.

I GUESS HE'S IN SUCH A TIGHT SPOT THAT HE'D WELCOME THE HELP OF ANYONE WHO CAN DO MATH, EVEN A CHILD?

I MEAN, BESIDES ALL THE PROBLEMS REGARDING CLASSIFIED INFORMATION, ISN'T IT PRETTY OUT THERE TO ASK A KID FOR HELP?

UM... IS THIS THE KIND OF OFFER I SHOULD ACCEPT?

WHA?

IF YOU KEEP TEACHING ME LETTERS AND GET REPLACE- MENT SLATE PENS FOR ME.

OKAY, I'LL HELP.

THOSE AREN'T TOO EXPENSIVE OR HARD TO GET.

SLATE PENS?

THAT'S FINE WITH ME, BUT...

I WANT TO LEARN TO READ, AND I WANT YOU TO TEACH ME.

...PROBABLY BECAUSE I PLAY WITH THE SLATE ALL DAY.

NO MATTER HOW MANY THEY BUY, I ALWAYS NEED MORE.

WHY'S THAT?

Ngh!

BUT NOW IT TAKES A LOT OF BEGGING FOR MOM TO GET ME ANY AT ALL.

MY PARENTS USED TO BUY THEM FOR ME.

A-ANY-WAY!

AHAHA...

...SLATE PENS ARE PRETTY CHEAP, BUT SURE.

Heheh.

IT'S A DEAL.

THE POINT IS,

I'M NOT A CHEAP ENOUGH GIRL TO WORK FOR FREE.

ドン

(Thump)

LOOKS LIKE YOU NEED TO HIRE SOME NEW SOLDIERS THAT KNOW MATH.

CAN YOU CHECK TO SEE IF THE MATH ON THESE SHEETS IS RIGHT?

WHAT SHOULD I DO?

BASI-CALLY, I DON'T KNOW WHERE THE ERRORS ARE, AND LOOKING FOR THEM TAKES ME A LOT OF TIME.

CHECKING ALL THE MATH HIM-SELF WAS QUITE THE TIME-CON-SUMING TASK.

PART OF HIS JOB WAS LOOKING THROUGH PAPER-WORK OTHERS HAD MADE.

...I WANT TO ASK, BUT MAYBE I'LL SAVE THAT FOR LATER.

I WONDER IF THERE'S SOME COMPLI-CATED CIRCUM-STANCES BEHIND OTTO BE-COMING A SOLDIER?

I ONLY GOT HIRED IN THE FIRST PLACE BECAUSE I CAN DO THIS KINDA STUFF.

THAT'D BE IDEAL, BUT...

HMM?

Ah.
MYNE, DO YOU WANT TO USE THE CALCULATOR?

コリ
(Scratch)

(Scratch)
コリ

NO THANKS. I DON'T KNOW HOW TO USE IT, ANYWAY.

IT'LL BE FASTER TO JUST WRITE OUT THE MATH THAN USE A FANTASY CALCULATOR I DON'T UNDERSTAND.

(Clink)
カチャ

ハラハラ

(Rustle)

GLAD TO BE OF SERVICE.

YOU HELPED SO MUCH!

I'M MOVED, HONESTLY.

Wow!

OH MAN, THIS IS GREAT!

77

WANT TO INTRODUCE YOU TO THE MER-CHANT'S GUILD?

IF YOU'RE THIS GOOD AT MATH, MYNE, YOU MIGHT JUST MAKE A GOOD MERCHANT.

...I'LL THINK ABOUT IT.

THEY COULD HELP WHEN I REACH THE POINT OF MASS PRODUCING BOOKS AND WANT TO START A BOOK-STORE.

IT MIGHT BE A GOOD IDEA TO MAKE CONNEC-TIONS IN THE MER-CHANT'S GUILD SOONER RATHER THAN LATER.

WELL, I MEAN, WRITING PAPER-WORK MEANS TOUCHING PARCH-MENT, RIGHT?

IT MEANS WRITING LETTERS WITH INK, DOESN'T IT?

REA-LLY?!

THAT WAY YOU CAN HELP ME WITH WRITING PAPER-WORK NEXT YEAR.

YOU KNOW, I THINK I'LL TAKE TEACH-ING YOU LETTERS PRETTY SERIOUS-LY.

HUH?

IS THAT SOME-THING TO BE HAPPY ABOUT?

ぱぁ、
(Shine)

(Tap) (Tap)

YEEES!

HOW COULD I NOT BE HAPPY?!

THIS IS THE OUTFIT FOR TUULI'S BAPTISM CEREMONY?

WOOOW!

OKAY, ALL FINISHED.

I THINK IT WOULD BE EVEN CUTER IF SHE ADDED MORE FRILLS AND DECORATION.

IT'S CUTE, DEFINITELY, BUT...

MHM. CUTE, ISN'T IT?

OH, TUULI. WHAT ABOUT YOUR HAIR?

THOUGH IT MIGHT BE IMPROPER TO WEAR FLASHY CLOTHING DURING A RELIGIOUS CEREMONY, I DON'T KNOW.

く3。
(Spin)

く3
(Spin)

OKAY, ARE YOU GOING TO PUT ON A HAIR ORNAMENT?

NO, BUT... I WAS JUST PLANNING TO WEAR IT LIKE THIS.

ARE THERE ANY RULES ABOUT HAVING TO WEAR YOUR HAIR A CERTAIN WAY?

I'LL TAKE CARE OF THIS!

I'LL MAKE YOU LOOK SUPER CUTE, I SWEAR!

BUT...

MMM, MY CEREMONY IS IN THE SUMMER, SO MAYBE I'LL PICK A FLOWER.

DON'T DO THAT!

IT'D BE A WASTE OF YOUR CUTE OUTFIT!

WH-WHAT SHOULD I DO?

THE NEEDLE MY MOM HAS FOR WOOL IS WAY TOO THICK...

I LEARNED TO DO ARTS AND CRAFTS THANKS TO MY OLD MOM ALWAYS BE—

(Clench)

IF SHE DOESN'T HAVE A HAIRPIN, I'LL JUST HAVE TO MAKE HER ONE MY-SELF.

I DON'T HAVE A NEEDLE FOR SEWING LACE!

Ah!

HE'S MY ONLY HOPE...

I NEED A THINNER NEEDLE...

YOU'RE PRETTY GOOD WITH YOUR HANDS, AREN'T YOU?

TUULI TOLD ME THAT YOU CARVED HER DOLL FOR HER.

ムグ (sip)

Hm?

YEAH, I GUESS I AM.

WHAT?

U-UM, WELL...

DAD.

(Step)

ハ ハ (Step)

82

NUH UH.

I WANT A SEWING NEEDLE.

Ahem.

AHHH, WHAT, DO YOU WANT A DOLL TOO?

I NEED ONE THAT'S A LOT, LOT THINNER.

NO, NOT LIKE HERS!

I'LL BE USING IT TO WEAVE THREAD THAT'S A LOT THIN-NER THAN WOOL.

は (Haaah)

(Wave)

(Wave)

JUST BORROW HERS, THEN.

A SEWING NEEDLE?

LIKE THE KIND EFFA USES?

DADDY, I THINK MAKING A THIN NEEDLE WILL BE SUUUPER HARD.

BUT COULD YOU DO IT ANYWAY, JUST FOR ME?

(Clatter)

YOU'RE AMAZING, DAD!

...WOOD'LL BE FINE, RIGHT?

(Scrape)

(Scrape)

COULD YOU MAKE IT THINNER?

ABOUT THIS MUCH?

...MYNE.

MHM, ME TOO.

I'm so glad. DAD'S SURE LOOKING HAPPIER NOW.

(Twist)

(Twist)

CAN I HAVE SOME OF THIS COLORED THREAD?

MOM.

...FOR WHAT?

WELL, IT WAS MY FAULT HE WAS IN A BAD MOOD, BUT...

ALL'S WELL THAT ENDS WELL.

SO I CAN MAKE TUULI'S HAIRPIN, I MEAN.

I'M GOING TO SEW SOME [LACE].

DON'T BE RIDI-CULOUS! THE CUTER, THE BETTER!

CUTENESS IS JUSTICE!

WE DON'T NEED TO TRY AND MAKE TUULI LOOK CUTER THAN SHE ALREADY IS.

(Clench)

A HAIRPIN? WON'T SHE ONLY USE THAT DURING THE BAPTISM CERE-MONY?

IT WOULD BE A WASTE TO USE THREAD ON SOME-THING LIKE THAT.

Ah!

I'M NOT SURE WHAT YOU MEAN BY THAT, BUT DON'T BACK-TALK YOUR MOTHER.

85

(Gasp!)

JUST THIS EXTRA THREAD WILL BE ENOUGH!

I WANT TO USE THE NEEDLE DAD'S MAKING FOR ME!

...IT'S NOT EVERY DAY MYNE GETS INTERESTED IN SEWING. WHAT'S THE HARM IN GIVING HER A LITTLE THREAD?

.....

EHEEEH.

THANKS, MOM! I LOVE YOU, DAD!

YOU HAVE A POINT.

Sigh.

86

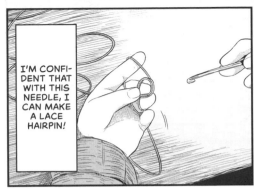

I'M CONFI-DENT THAT WITH THIS NEEDLE, I CAN MAKE A LACE HAIRPIN!

TO THINK THAT OUT OF ALL THE ARTS AND CRAFTS I DID AS URANO, LACE SEWING WOULD END UP BEING THE MOST USEFUL TO ME.

(Tighten) すぃ (Tighten) すぃ

(Spin) くる

(Scoot) せっ (Scoot) せっ

(Scoot) せっ (Scoot) せっ

ISN'T THAT A LITTLE SMALL?

コロ (Roll)

WANT TO TRY?

YOU'RE MORE USED TO SEWING THAN I AM, MOM.

YOU'LL PROBABLY BE A LOT BETTER THAN ME AT THIS.

I'LL BUNDLE UP A LOT OF SMALL FLOWERS TO MAKE THE HAIR-PIN.

...THOSE DON'T SEEM TOO HARD TO MAKE.

.....

(Stare)

SHE CAN TELL HOW TO SEW THEM HERSELF JUST BY LOOKING AT THE FINISHED FLOWER.

WOW. BEHOLD, A TRUE SEWING BEAUTY.

プスプス (Sew)

88

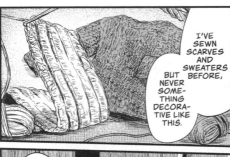

I'VE SEWN SCARVES AND SWEATERS BEFORE, BUT NEVER SOMETHING DECORATIVE LIKE THIS.

YOU'RE AMAZING, MOM.

WHAT'S AMAZING IS THAT YOU KNEW HOW TO MAKE THESE IN THE FIRST PLACE.

...SO, HOW WILL YOU ATTACH THESE TOGETHER?

...WAIT, THE [PIN]?!

は (Gasp!)

UMMM, WELL.

I'LL MAKE A CIRCLE OUT OF CLOTH

AND SEW THEM ONTO IT.

NO WAY WOULD SOMETHING THAT USEFUL EXIST IN THIS WORLD!

D-D-DAAAD!

CAN YOU MAKE A TINY HAIR STICK WITH ONE POINTED END AND A FLAT END,

わた
(Panic)

わた
(Panic)

WITH A SMALL HOLE ON THE FLAT END? I REALLY NEED ONE!

...HEHEH.

ぱっ
(Shine)

HEH. WELL, THAT'D BE EASIER THAN THE NEEDLE I JUST MADE.

REA-LLY?!

I WIN, OTTO.

(Squeeze)

ぎゅっ

YOU'RE AMAZING, DAD!

I'VE NEVER RE-SPECTED ANYTHING THIS MUCH BEFORE IN MY LIFE!

(Achoo!)

ズイル
(Pull)

TUULI, SIT, SIT. I'LL BRAID YOUR HAIR.

YUP! SUPER CUTE!

キゅっ
(Squeeze)

NEVER SEEN A CUTER GIRL IN MY LIFE, TUULI!

THOSE BRAIDS ARE VERY CUTE,

AND THE HAIRPIN'S COLORS LOOK JUST PERFECT ON YOU.

REALLY?

WOW...

THANK YOU, EVERYONE!

I'M SO HAPPY!

WELL... NOT THAT I MIND.

BEFORE I KNEW IT, THE NEEDLE DAD MADE FOR ME WAS FIT SNUGLY INTO HER SEWING BOX.

THE NEXT DAY,

I LEARNED THAT MOM HAD GOTTEN ADDICTED TO LACE SEWING.

Ch.8: Helping Out Otto End

Ch.9 Bring Me to the Forest

(Scoop)

(Scoop)

(Step) (Step)

I'M BACK, MYNE!

WEL-COME BACK, TUULI.

OH? YOU GOT SOME KRANS?

(Step)

(Step)

SO BASICAL-LY... IT'S ALMOST SPRING?

UH HUH, 'CAUSE THE SNOW'S MELTING IN THE FOREST TOO.

THERE'S STILL NOT MUCH TO GATHER THERE, THOUGH.

I CAN FINALLY MAKE CLAY TABLETS!

(Ta-dah!)

NO WAY. YOU CAN'T WALK THAT FAR.

HEY, TUULI!

COULD YOU TAKE ME TO THE FOREST WITH YOU?

LET'S SEE WHAT DAD HAS TO SAY.

.....

I'VE GOTTEN A LITTLE STRONGER!

PLEASE!

ぎゅっ (Grab)

うぅーーん (Hmmm)

YOU, GOING TO THE FOREST?

LET'S SEE HERE...

I MEAN, I ONLY ENDED UP STUCK IN BED FIVE TIMES THIS WINTER!

...OH, AND JUST SO YOU KNOW, THAT'S A LOT LESS THAN USUAL.

バッバッ (Wave)

I BARELY GET FEVERS ANYMORE, RIGHT?

(Clench)

I CAN DO IT!

I'LL BE FINE!

NOT ONLY THAT, BUT I'VE BEEN EATING DECENT MEALS MORE OFTEN, AND MY BODY'S BIGGER THAN BEFORE.

Food

EXER-CISE!

One! Two! Three! Four! Five! Six! Seven!

Building Stamina

SURE, BUT...

THOSE ARE KIDS THAT RAMPAGE AROUND THE HOUSE 'CAUSE THEY'VE GOT SO MUCH ENERGY. THEY'RE GETTING KICKED OUT FOR THE DAY.

I'LL REST AT THE GATE IF I REALLY CAN'T HANDLE IT, OKAY?

OKAY?

PLEASE.

(Tug)

I MEAN, THERE ARE THREE-YEAR-OLDS THAT GO TO THE FOREST ALREADY, AREN'T THERE?

(Scratch)

(Scratch)

EEEH...

DON'T BE STUPID!

YOU DON'T NEED TO THROW A TANTRUM!

(Raise) Z...

SO BASICALLY, IF I THROW A TANTRUM YOU'LL LET ME GO?

WHAT CAN I DO THAT WILL CONVINCE YOU I'LL BE OKAY?

...DAD, YOU'RE WORRIED BECAUSE I'M SO WEAK, RIGHT?

WHAT CAN I DO?

(Scratch) ボリボリ
(Scratch)

LET'S SEE...

WHEN YOU CAN REACH THE GATE WITHOUT LAGGING BEHIND EVERYONE, YOU CAN GO TO THE FOREST.

WALK TO THE GATE FOR NOW.

AS EXPECTED, HE WOULDN'T LET ME GO SO EASILY.

...OKAY.

HEY, DAD.

BY "WALK TO THE GATE," DO YOU MEAN WALK THERE AND BACK TOO?

TCH. I REALLY WANTED TO GO TO THE FOREST.

MY CLAY TABLETS...

WHA?

...YOU DON'T MIND?

NAH...

YOU CAN STAY AT THE GATE AND LEARN YOUR LETTERS FROM OTTO.

(Chew)

(Chew)

...WHAT KIND OF JOBS ARE WE TALKING ABOUT?

OTTO SAID YOU'D DO GREAT AT A JOB WHERE YOU USE YOUR HEAD.

IF YOU LEARN YOUR LETTERS, YOU CAN FIND A COZIER JOB THAN HARD LABOR STUFF.

BUT YOU'RE SMART.

YOU'RE REAL WEAK AND SICKLY, YEAH?

YOU'LL GET MORE MONEY THAT WAY, AND IT'LL BE EASIER ON YOUR BODY.

HE SAID THAT YOU COULD BE A WRITER THAT WRITES DOCUMENTS FOR OFFICES AND NOBLES.

YOU COULD SAVE WORK FOR WHEN YOU'RE FEELING HEALTHY.

WELL.

OTTO'S A SOLDIER NOW, BUT HE USED TO BE A TRAVELING MERCHANT.

HE STILL HAS CONNECTIONS IN THE MERCHANT'S GUILD.

WRITING DOCUMENTS FOR SOMEONE ELSE WOULD BE KIND OF LIKE WHAT PARALEGALS DO, I GUESS?

ドッ (Staaare) ん…

ポフ (Pat)

YOUR MOTHER AND I DON'T HAVE MANY JOBS WE COULD GET YOU, SO...

DON'T WASTE YOUR CONNECTION TO OTTO, ALRIGHT?

...THANKS, DAD.

I'LL DO MY BEST.

...DAD WAS SUPER LAME WHEN HE WAS JEALOUS OF OTTO, BUT NOW HE'S BEING SUPER COOL!

TUULI. WILL YOU HELP HER?

...MYNE CAN'T DO IT.

BUT SHE HAS TO GET STRONG ENOUGH TO VISIT THE FOREST SOMEDAY.

I KNOW. NOT NOW.

THAT'S TRUE, BUT...

...SHE'LL GET IN THE WAY.

(Tug)
(Tug)

RIGHT NOW, SHE'S GETTING IN EVERYONE'S WAY.

YEP.

I'LL ASK LUTZ TO HELP HER GET HOME ON THE WAY BACK.

I'LL WALK WITH MYNE UNTIL SHE'S STRONG ENOUGH TO GET TO THE GATE.

(Squeeze)

SO, WHEN MYNE GETS STRONG ENOUGH TO WALK TO THE GATE,

I WANT YOU TO HELP TOO, TUULI.

OK THEN. I'LL HELP.

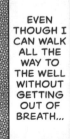

EVEN THOUGH I CAN WALK ALL THE WAY TO THE WELL WITHOUT GETTING OUT OF BREATH...

THEY DON'T EVEN THINK I CAN WALK TO THE GATE.

...OH.

DON'T PUSH YOUR- SELF TOO HARD, OKAY?

YEAH, OF COURSE.

GUN- THER, KEEP AN EYE ON HER.

LET'S GO.

I'LL BE BACK!

ビュン゛!゛
(Fwip)

(Crunch)
ザッ

(Crunch)
ザッ

...YOU OKAY, MYNE?

(Heave)
ぜぇ
(Heave)
ぜぇ

(Haah)
はぁ

(Heave)
ぜぇ

(Haah)
はぁ

は
(Haah)

は
(Haah)

...I'M, STILL...

は
(Haah)

JUST,

FINE...

は
(Haah)

は
(Haah)

UP YOU GO.

ひょいっ
(Lift)

Sigh.

YOU DON'T LOOK LIKE IT.

MY FAMILY WAS RIGHT!

I CAN'T GO TO THE FOREST!

ゼエ
(Heave)

OKAY, THIS IS TOO MUCH!

I FEEL LIKE DEATH!

はぁ
(Haaah)

ぐぅ
(Squeeeze)

WHAT ABOUT HIS OWN WORK?

RIGHT.

WE HAVE FIVE APPRENTICES THAT FINISHED THEIR SPRING BAPTISMS.

HEY, DAD.

I WAS WONDERING ABOUT OTTO TEACHING ME LETTERS.

DOES HE REALLY HAVE THE TIME TO DO THAT?

ASSIST-ANT?

BUT YOU'RE NOT AN APPRENTICE SOLDIER, YOU'RE HIS ASSISTANT.

YEAH, PRETTY MUCH.

IT'S OTTO'S JOB TO TEACH THEM TO READ.

SO HE'S GOING TO TEACH ME WITH THEM?

OTTO'S BEEN SAYING FOR A LONG TIME NOW THAT THERE'S TOO MUCH WORK FOR HIM TO DO ALONE,

BUT NOBODY HERE KNOWS ENOUGH MATH TO HELP HIM.

HE WANTS TO TEACH YOU TO READ AND MAKE YOU HIS ASSISTANT.

MYNE, YOU'VE BEEN HELPING HIM WORK, RIGHT?

UH HUH, WITH HIS BUDGET REPORTS AND STUFF...

BUT THAT WAS ALL.

YOU'RE BASICALLY BEING HIRED, BUT WE CAN'T GIVE WORK TO A CHILD THAT HASN'T BEEN BAPTIZED YET.

I GUESS HE WASN'T JOKING WHEN HE SAID HE WANTED ME AS HIS ASSISTANT.

AT THE TIME, I JUST TOOK HIM TEACHING ME LETTERS AS PAYMENT FOR ME HELPING HIM, BUT...

YOU CAN TAKE DAYS OFF WHEN YOU GET SICK.

YOUR PAYMENT WILL BE SLATE PENS.

SO ON THE OUTSIDE, YOU'RE GOING TO THE GATE JUST TO BE TAUGHT YOUR LETTERS.

OTTO'S MANAGED TO GET THE MOST BENEFIT FOR HIMSELF WHILE SPENDING THE LEAST AMOUNT OF MONEY. JUST WHAT I'D EXPECT FROM A FORMER MERCHANT.

SO BASICALLY, HE'S TEACHING ME LETTERS NOW IN RETURN FOR ME HELPING HIM WITH WORK...

AND ALL OF THIS IS PREPARATION FOR NEXT YEAR'S BUDGET SEASON?

OTTO WAS REAL CONVINCING WHEN HE SAID WE WOULDN'T FIND A CHEAPER ASSISTANT FOR HIM THAN YOU.

HEYA, MYNE.

I'M JUST ABOUT TO START. ARE YOU ALL REST- ED UP?

UH HUH, I'M FINE.

コッ (Step)
コッ (Step)

THOSE MUST BE THE APPREN- TICES DAD MEN- TIONED.

Training Room

キィ (Creak)

THIS GIRL IS MYNE. SHE'S THE DAUGHTER OF THIS SECTION'S CAPTAIN, AND SHE'S HELPING ME WITH PAPERWORK.

SHE'S HERE TODAY TO LEARN LETTERS WITH YOU ALL.

LOOKS LIKE EVERYONE'S HERE.

YES SIR!

GOOD, LET'S GET STARTED.

DON'T EVEN THINK ABOUT PLAYING ANY PRANKS ON HER.

ゴ (Rattle) トリ

THESE ARE THE THIRTY-FIVE LETTERS OF THE ALPHABET.

WE'LL LEARN THEM FIVE AT A TIME AND PRACTICE PRONOUNCING THEM.

コツ (Scrap)

コツ (Scrape)

112

(Scratch)

(Scratch)

(Scratch)

(Scratch)

ガタ
(Scoot)

I'M SURE FOR MOST OF THESE KIDS, IT'S THEIR FIRST TIME EVEN HOLDING A SLATE PEN.

そわ
(Fidget)

そわ
(Fidget)

UNLIKE OTHER KIDS IN THIS WORLD, I'M USED TO SITTING DOWN AND STUDY- ING.

I DON'T DISLIKE THE ACT OF LEARN- ING.

I LIKE THIS KIND OF STUFF MORE THAN RUNNING AROUND.

...MYNE, YOU REALLY ARE A FAST LEARNER.

114

HUH? ALREADY?

YOU KNOW, OTTO, I THINK YOU SHOULD WRAP UP THE LESSON SOON.

TEACH THEM THE MORAL CODE OF A SOLDIER.

THEN HAVE THEM DRAW SKETCHES OF THE CITY STREETS.

YOU SHOULD TEACH LETTERS FOR A BIT, THEN MOVE ON TO MATH.

MIX IN SOME EXERCISE.

(Fwip)

フイ

THESE KIDS ARE HOLDING SLATE PENS FOR THE FIRST TIME. THEY CAN'T FOCUS FOR THAT LONG.

(Scratch) カリ カリ (Scratch)

NOT TO MENTION THAT KIDS IN THIS WORLD AREN'T USED TO SITTING DOWN FOR VERY LONG, SO IT'S EVEN HARDER FOR THEM.

EVEN A JAPANESE ELEMENTARY SCHOOLER COULDN'T SURVIVE A WHOLE DAY OF MEMORIZING JUST HIRAGANA.

BASICALLY, YOU SHOULD DO ALL SORTS OF THINGS AND HAVE THEM LEARN BIT BY BIT.

JUST LIKE ELEMENTARY SCHOOLS THAT CHANGE CLASSES EVERY HOUR.

.....

LET'S DO MATH NEXT.

AFTER THIRTY MINUTES... ACTUALLY, NO.

ONCE THEY START GETTING FIDGETY AND LOSE FOCUS, YOU SHOULD CHANGE THE SUBJECT TO SOMETHING ELSE.

(Dash)

SCHOOL'S OUT!

THAT'S ENOUGH STUDYING FOR TODAY!

(Clap)

...MYNE, I DON'T THINK THEY'LL LEARN MUCH IF YOU GO THAT EASY ON THEM.

IF EVEN ONE OF YOU DOESNS'T HAVE THEM MEMORIZED, IT'LL SLOW EVERYONE ELSE DOWN.

BE SURE TO PRACTICE THE LETTERS AND NUMBERS YOU LEARNED TODAY!

MEMORIZING THEM IS AN IMPORTANT PART OF YOUR JOB.

OKAY!

...MR. OTTO, YOU SHOULDN'T COMPARE ME WITH THEM.

AH... RIGHT.

BUT IF YOU FORCE THEM TO STUDY TOO MUCH, THEY'LL START TO HATE LEARNING.

MMM?

I THINK WHAT WE DID TODAY WAS GOOD ENOUGH TO AVOID THAT.

THAT'LL BE THEIR RESPONSIBILITY.

THAT'S NOT GOING EASY ON THEM, RIGHT?

ニコ

(Smile)

PLUS, IF THEY DON'T MEMORIZE WHAT WE LEARNED TODAY, YOU CAN KEEP THEM HERE UNTIL THEY HAVE.

ANYWAY, TIME FOR YOUR OWN LESSONS, MYNE.

OKAY!

EXPECTING RESPONSIBILITY FROM KIDS WHO JUST STARTED WORK IS A BIT MUCH, BUT SURE.

Haha.

LET TERS?

YOU CAN WRITE?!

LEARN-ING MY LET-TERS.

WHAT WERE YOU DOING AT THE GATE, MYNE?

ぱ°(Shine)あ、

YOU CAN WRITE YOUR OWN NAME!

WOAH, MYNE! THAT'S AMA-ZING!

ONLY MY NAME RIGHT NOW.

I'M STILL LEARNING.

サク (Crunch)

サク (Crunch)

I WAS THINK-ING ANY KID SHOULD BE ABLE TO WRITE THEIR OWN NAME, BUT I GUESS BEING LITERATE AT ALL IS ACTU-ALLY RARE IN THIS WORLD.

WHA?

はぁ (Häah)

はぁ (Häah)

ワ ll (Chatter)

EVERY-ONE'S...

...SO FAST...

ワ ll (Chatter)

I THINK I CAN UNDER-STAND WHY BEING ABLE TO HELP WITH PAPER-WORK IS SUCH A BIG DEAL HERE.

NOW I KNOW WHY OTTO WANTS ME TO BE HIS ASSISTANT.

COULD YOU TAKE CARE OF MYNE FOR ME?

I HAVE TO GET EVERY-ONE ELSE HOME!

SURE, LEAVE IT TO ME.

SORRY, LUTZ!

SORRY!

タ (Dash)

YOU OKAY?

(Wobble)

WALK AS SLOW AS YOU NEED TO, MYNE.

...THANKS.

は あ… (Haah)

GETTING STRONGER IS HARD.

...LEARNING LETTERS IS EASY, BUT...

I'LL STICK WITH YOU, SO DON'T WORRY.

ポ ー (Clasp)

YOU CAN DO IT, MYNE.

AND I'M GONNA HAVE TO WALK THIS FAR TO-MORROW, TOO...

I'M HOME!

(Creak)

(Gleam)

I WENT TO THE GATE FIVE DAYS IN A ROW THIS WEEK!

YOU SHOULD BE ABLE TO GO TO THE FOREST SOON.

YOU'VE GOTTEN SO MUCH STRONGER.

YOU DID IT, MYNE! THIS IS THE FIRST TIME YOU DIDN'T HAVE TO REST!

は (Haah)

は (Haah)

UH HUH!

(Steam)

...UM?

122

...LOOKS LIKE YOU STILL ENDED UP WITH A FEVER.

BUT STILL, I'M IMPRESSED.

YOU USED TO JUST SPEND ALL DAY CRYING ABOUT HOW ONLY TUULI GETS TO GO OUTSIDE.

NOW YOU'RE WORKING HARD.

GOOD JOB, MYNE.

YOU CAN'T SLEEP?

OKAY, I'LL TELL YOU SOME STORIES.

.....

...ANOTHER ONE ABOUT THE KIDS FROM THE STARS?

OH, DO YOU WANT TO HEAR ANOTHER ONE?

123

...NO.

THAT ONE'S FINE.

BY THE TIME THEY GAVE ME PERMISSION TO GO TO THE FOREST,

SPRING WAS ENDING AND THE FIRST HINTS OF SUMMER WERE BEGINNING TO SHOW.

THREE MONTHS PASSED SINCE I STARTED WALKING TO THE GATE.

Ch.9: Bring Me to the Forest End

(Duuuuuuun!)

Ch.10 Finally the Forest

(Dun)

(Dun)

YOUR GOAL IS TO REST THERE AND COME BACK WITH EVERYONE ELSE.

GOT IT?

YOU'RE JUST GOING TO THE FOREST AND COMING BACK TODAY.

I KNOW.

MYNE.

(Swipe) (Swipe)

125

TALK WITH LUTZ ABOUT HELPING MYNE GET HOME.

TUULI, IT'S GONNA BE ROUGH, BUT I'M COUNTING ON YOU.

.....

I'LL MAKE SURE WE LEAVE EARLY TODAY.

UH HUH.

I THINK TUULI'S GOING TO BE EXTRA HARSH TODAY.

You can count on me!

THIS IS MY FIRST TIME GOING TO THE FOREST.

Walk as slow as you need to.

ALRIGHT MYNE, LET'S GO.

UH HUH.

ALL THANKS TO LUTZ KEEPING AN EYE ON MY PACE.

I CAN WALK TO THE GATE JUST FINE NOW,

IT REALLY BROUGHT OUT THE PARUE'S SWEET-NESS, DIDN'T IT?

Parue Burger

THE PARUE BURGERS YOU MADE THE OTHER DAY WERE SOMETHIN' ELSE...

Mhm. Mhm.

I MEAN, GUNTHER'S PAYING ME A LITTLE FOR THIS, SO...

AND YOU'RE HELPING ME OUT TOO.

(Smile)

THANKS FOR ALL YOUR HELP, LUTZ!

ガッシガッシガッ

PLUS, IT'S REALLY HARD TO CHOP IT UP LIKE THAT.

YOU NEED FRESH MEAT TO MINCE IT, DON'T YOU?

WHY DIDN'T YOU TEACH US HOW TO MAKE THOSE DURING THE WIN-TER?

I DIDN'T KNOW IF YOU'D ALL BE WILLING TO HELP ME.

Lots of Manual Labor

(Heave) (Heave)

AAAH... YEAH, IT WAS PRETTY ROUGH.

BUT YOUR FOOD'S WORTH THE WORK.

ALRIGHT, I'M GONNA GO GET FIREWOOD. YOU STAY HERE AND REST.

NOW THAT I'VE COME TO THE FOREST, COULD I BEAR TO GO HOME WITHOUT DOING ANYTHING?

(Step)

NO, I COULD NOT!

(Tada!)

I'M GONNA DIG MY HEART OUT!

I'M GONNA DIG.

(Charge!)

COME ON OUT, STICKY CLAY!

(Whoosh)

HYAH!

(Thump!)

I MEAN, IT FEELS LIKE THE GROUND OF A SPORTS ARENA.

SERIOUSLY? CAN YOU EVEN DIG INTO THIS?

SO HARD!

(Paaang!)

(Clatter)

MAN, I THOUGHT FOREST GROUND WOULD BE SOFT AND MOIST...

I'M GONNA DIG BIT BY BIT!

...BUT I WON'T GIVE UP.

(Squeeze)

(Scratch)

(Scratch)

(Scratch)

(Scratch)

(Scratch)

MYNE?

(Rustle)

(Twitch!)

WHAT ARE YOU DOING?

UM...

(Stomp)

YOU PROMISED NOT TO DO ANYTHING IN THE FOREST THAT'D TIRE YOU OUT, REMEMBER?!

(Clatter)

(Clatter)

(Tremble)

BUT, WELL, UM.

LUTZ.

(Tremble)

UM.

(Tremble)

(Rumble)

(Rumble)

...BUT WHAT?

(Loom)

I TOLD YOU TO REST. WHAT DO YOU THINK YOU'RE DOING?

I CAN SEE THAT.

WHY ARE YOU DIGGING?

I-I'M...

DIGGING HOLES!

...UMM, WELL.

I WANT [STICKY CLAY].

(Fidget)
おず、、

GOOD TO KNOW!

(Beam)
ぱぁ、、

...THERE IS MORE GROUND LIKE THAT OVER THERE THAN WHERE YOU ARE.

HUH? YOU WANT WHAT?

UM... LIKE, GROUND THAT'S HEAVY, ALL BAD AT DRAINING WATER,

AND ALL CLUMPED TOGETHER. STICKY.

C'MON MYNE, HOLD ON!

Ah!

THANKS, LUTZ!

IF I DON'T DIG IT MYSELF, WHO WILL?!

DON'T GET MAD AT ME! MY FAMILY DOESN'T CARE ABOUT THIS STUFF AT ALL!

(Jerk)

OWOW!

(Squeeze)

YOUR JOB TODAY IS TO REST.

ARE YOU DEAF OR SOMETHING?

WHA...?

SO JUST SIT STILL AND REST.

Fine...

...I'LL DIG IT FOR YOU ONCE I FINISH GATHERING MY FIREWOOD.

.....

YOU'RE TOO WEAK TO DIG ON YOUR OWN. I'LL DO IT FOR YOU.

BUT IN RETURN,

I WANT YOU TO TELL ME WHAT YOU'RE GOING TO USE IT FOR.

...UM, I APPRECI-ATE THE THOUGHT, BUT...

SHOULDN'T YOU FOCUS ON WHAT YOU NEED YOURSELF?

I CAN SAVE MYSELF EFFORT IF I KNOW EXACTLY WHAT YOU WANT.

...WHY?

トー (tap)
トー (tap)

NGH...

YOU WERE JUST DIG-GING AT THE WRONG SPOT EVEN THOUGH YOU KNEW WHAT KIND OF EARTH YOU WANTED, YEAH?

...WHY ARE YOU HELPING ME, LUTZ?

WHEN YOU DID THAT,

I DECIDED TO HELP YOU WHEN YOU NEEDED IT.

YOU MADE PARUE CAKES FOR ME WHEN I WAS HUNGRY, YEAH?

HE'S HELPING ME DIG UP CLAY JUST FOR THAT?

...I GUESS GOOD FOOD IS A POWERFUL MOTIVATOR.

ALRIGHT, I'M GONNA GO GET SOME WOOD.

WHAT...? JUST FOR THAT?

AROUND HERE SHOULD BE GOOD.

ザッ
(Scrap)

...INTENTIONALLY BROUGHT IT...

ピク
(Twitch)

だら
(Waver)
だら
(Waver)

I WAS JUST SO EXCITED TO GO TO THE FOREST.

I JUST COULDN'T HELP MYSELF, AND...

W-WELL, THAT'S JUST... UM.

YOU WERE NEVER GONNA KEEP THAT PROMISE, WERE YOU?

Y'KNOW, SINCE YOU BROUGHT THIS THING WITH YOU...

ザクッ
(Crunch)

I THINK YOU SHOULD LET YOUR GUARD DOWN A BIT MORE... WHY DO YOU HAVE TO BE SMARTER THAN MY DAD?

MR. GUNTHER'S JUST TOO SOFT ON YOU!

ザクッ
(Crunch)

YOU LOOK ALL NICE AND SWEET ON THE OUTSIDE, BUT I CAN NEVER LET MY GUARD DOWN AROUND YOU!

COME OOON!

(Lift)

HAAAH...

THIS IS WHAT YOU WANT, RIGHT?

THERE'S NOT A GUY ALIVE WHO'S NOT STRONGER THAN YOU.

(Shovel)

(Shovel)

YOU'RE AMAZING, LUTZ! SO STRONG!

(Knead) (Knead)

IT WOULD HAVE TAKEN ME DAYS TO GET THIS MUCH.

YES, THIS IS IT!

Eheheh~

I'M GONNA MAKE [CLAY TABLETS].

SO.

WHAT DO YOU WANT IT FOR?

WATCH.

FIRST I GOTTA MOLD IT INTO SHAPE...

(Squeeze)

(Squeeze)

SAY WHAT NOW?

(Scrape)

UH HUH.

YOU CARVE LETTERS INTO IT AND RECORD INFORMATION.

...ARE THOSE LETTERS?

(Scrape)

(Scrape)

BOOKS ARE COMPILATIONS OF RECORDED INFORMATION, AND THEY'RE EVEN MORE AMAZING!

BY RECORDING INFORMATION, YOU CAN REMEMBER IT LATER EVEN IF YOU FORGET.

ISN'T THAT AMAZING?

カリ
(Scritch)

I'M GOING TO BE WRITING FOR A WHILE....

AL-RIGHT...

THANKS FOR DIGGING OUT THE CLAY FOR ME, LUTZ.

THAT'S ALL THE HELP I'LL NEED RIGHT NOW.

CLAY TABLETS ARE AMAZING! I'M SO GLAD I FINISHED THEM!

LONG LIVE THE MIGHTY MESOPOTAMIAN CULTURE!

YAAAY! ALL DONE!

140

NOW I JUST NEED TO TAKE THEM HOME AND BAKE TH—

(Spin)

GY

(Squash)

HOW HARD DO YOU THINK I WORKED TO GET TO THE FOREST?!

HOW HARD DO YOU THINK IT WAS TO GET THIS WEAK BODY STRONG ENOUGH TO GO TO THE FOREST...?!

MYNE?!

UWA AAA AAH!

I EVEN GOT TUULI AND LUTZ INVOLVED TO FINISH THEM!

YOU LOOK REALLY SCARY RIGHT NOW!

タタッ (Rush)

WHAT'S WRONG?

I DON'T CARE IF THEY THINK I'M BEING IMMATURE,

ギロッ (Glare)

FEY AND HIS FRIENDS STEPPED ON THE TABLET THINGS MYNE WS MAKING.

(Poke)
(Poke)
つん
つん

THIS WAS MY FIRST STEP TOWARDS MAKING ONE, AND YET...

MY LOVE FOR BOOKS WILL NEVER DIE,

NUH UH! I'LL NEVER FORGIVE THEM!

YOU SHO- ULDN'T BE CRY- ING SO HARD, MYNE.

THEY DIDN'T MEAN TO STEP ON THEM.

Grrr!

YEAH, WE'LL HELP! SORRY, SERIOUSLY!

I'LL HELP, AND I'M PRETTY SURE THEY WILL TOO.

(Nod) (Nod)

HEY, MYNE. I GET THAT YOU'RE MAD AND FRUSTRATED.

BUT GETTING ANGRY WON'T MAKE THEM COME BACK.

YOU'VE JUST GOT TO MAKE THEM AGAIN.

(Wipe)

.....

MYYYNE...

JUST A LITTLE LONGER...

MYNE. WE NEED TO GET GOING SOON.

146

I'LL HELP THE NEXT TIME WE COME TO THE FOREST TOO. YOU CAN FINISH THEM THEN.

...NO POINT IN ALL THIS IF WE CAN'T EVEN MAKE IT HOME.

OKAY? LET'S CALL IT QUITS FOR TODAY.

ガサ (Rustle)

ガサ (Rustle)

SHOULD BE FINE IF YOU PUT EVERY- THING THERE.

.....

OKAY.

...THANKS, LUTZ.

...YOU SURE HAVE IT ROUGH, TUULI.

YOU TOO, LUTZ.

MHM... I DON'T KNOW WHAT TO SAY TO DAD.

SHE'S PROBABLY GONNA GET A FEVER AND END UP STUCK IN BED FOR THREE DAYS LIKE THAT.

CLAAAY

(Sob) (Sob)

I WENT HOME AND JUST LIKE LUTZ PREDICTED,

MY ANGER ENDED UP GETTING ME SICK IN BED FOR THREE DAYS WITH A FEVER.

LATER THAT DAY

Hmph.

GOT IT? YOU NEED TO REST IN BED TODAY.

THREE DAYS LATER

YOU DON'T LOOK NEARLY HEALTHY ENOUGH TO GO TO THE FOREST TODAY!

NOT A CHANCE!

ANY-THING BUT THAT!

(PLOP)

AND THE NEXT TIME YOU BREAK A PROMISE, I'M REALLY GONNA BAN YOU FROM GOING TO THE FOREST!

GET READY, CLAY TAB-LETS.

I'M GONNA MAKE TONS AND TONS OF YOU!

BUT THAT MEANS I CAN GO TO THE FOREST IF I REST TODAY, RIGHT?

EHE-HEH.

149

(Whoosh)

THE NEXT DAY

WHY ARE YOU OPENING THE WINDOW, MYNE?!

RAIN?!

A STORM?!

NOOOOOOOOOOOOO!

(Whoosh)

THE FOREST!

WHERE DO YOU THINK YOU'RE GOING?!

(Grab)

MY CLAY TABLETS!

(Dash)

150

(Rub) 스ㅋ 스ㅋ (Rub)

Okaaaay...

Dry your hair, you'll catch a cold!

(Slump)

へこ

MY CLAY TABLETS...

NGH!

It's not happening!

YOU GET SICK AT THE DROP OF A HAT ALREADY! WHY WOULD YOU EVEN THINK ABOUT GOING OUTSIDE IN RAIN LIKE THIS?!

BY THE TIME I COULD GO TO THE FOREST AGAIN,

OVER A WEEK HAD PASSED SINCE I FIRST MADE MY CLAY TABLETS.

TUULI...

IT'LL BE OKAY.

EVERYONE SAID THEY'LL HELP YOU, SO THEY WON'T TAKE AS LONG TO MAKE THIS TIME.

THE STORM WAS A RARE LONGLASTING ONE.

151

I-I DIDN'T DO NOTHIN' THIS TIME!

THE RAIN DID THIS!

(Rub)

...LUTZ IS RIGHT.

(Pat)

IF YOU HAVE THE TIME TO CRY, YOU HAVE THE TIME TO MAKE MORE TABLETS.

...I KNOW THAT.

I FAILED THE THIRD TIME BECAUSE OF RAIN.

I FAILED THE SECOND TIME BECAUSE OF THE GATE'S CLOSING TIME.

I FAILED THE FIRST TIME BECAUSE OF FEY.

HEY, MYNE.

WHY BOTHER MAKING THESE ANYWAY?

I'VE BEEN THROUGH MAN-MADE AND NATURAL DISASTERS. THERE'S NOTHING THAT CAN GET IN MY WAY NOW.

I'LL FINISH THESE TABLETS, NO MATTER WHAT!

(Turn)

I MENTIONED IT A LITTLE BEFORE, BUT CLAY TABLETS ARE A MEDIUM FOR RECORDING INFORMATION.

(Squeeze)

(Squeeze)

YOU CAN SQUISH THEM INTO SHAPE AND WRITE LETTERS WITH YOUR FINGERS.

...YOU LOST ME.

Right?

YOU CAN BAKE THEM TO PRESERVE THEM TOO.

AREN'T THEY GREAT?

...UUUH.

SO BASICALLY, YOU WANT BOOKS?

I WANT TO GET ALL OF THEM AND SPEND MY LIFE READING THEM.

I WANT NEW BOOKS TO READ EVERY MONTH.

A STORY MY MOM TOLD ME.

I WON'T FORGET IT IF I RECORD IT, RIGHT?

SO, MYNE. WHAT'RE YOU WRITING?

NOT EXACTLY.

WHAT I REALLY WANT IS TO LIVE SURROUNDED BY BOOKS.

IS THAT WHAT YOU WANT TO DO, MYNE?

はぁ (Haah)

...AAAH, ALRIGHT, I GET IT.

BUT BOOKS AND PAPER ARE TOO EXPENSIVE FOR ME TO BUY, SO I HAVE TO MAKE THEM MYSELF.

BASICALLY, YES! SO BAD!

I WANT THEM RIGHT NOW!

RIGHT!

YOU'RE MAKING REPLACEMENT BOOKS RIGHT NOW, YEAH?

154

I'M GUESSING YOU ASKED ME THAT BECAUSE YOU HAVE SOMETHING YOU WANT TO DO YOURSELF?

SO, WHAT DO YOU WANT TO DO, LUTZ?

YOU KNOW HOW TRAVELING MERCHANTS AND MINSTRELS TRAVEL ALL OVER THE PLACE AND HAVE LOTS OF STORIES ABOUT PLACES?

I WANT TO SEE THOSE PLACES MYSELF TOO.

I WANT TO GO TO OTHER CITIES.

I...

YEAH.

...YOU REALLY THINK SO?

I'M TALKING ABOUT LEAVING THE CITY, Y'KNOW?

OH, THAT'S NICE. TRAVELING IS FUN.

FOR A LONG TIME MY DREAM WAS TO TRAVEL THE WORLD AND VISIT LOTS OF [LIBRARIES].

FOR A LONG TIME...

MHM.

WHY WOULDN'T IT BE FUN TO GO TO ALL SORTS OF PLACES?

WHY DON'T YOU DO WHAT YOU WANT TO TOO?

ニコ (Smile)

Man...

...NOW I FEEL DUMB FOR WORRYING.

YOU'RE ALWAYS DOING WHAT YOU WANT ANYWAY, MYNE.

...BUT NOW IT'LL NEVER COME TRUE.

......

156

...OKAY!

ヲ゛
(Dash)

THANKS FOR YOUR HELP!

Y-YEAH.

I ONLY NEEDED TEN OF THE CLAY TABLETS TO FINISH THE STORY,

SO YOU GUYS CAN GO GATHER NOW.

HMMM?

RALPH CAME TODAY, SO I'M GONNA STICK AROUND AND HELP YOU INSTEAD.

YOU'RE NOT GOING WITH THEM, LUTZ?

YOUR NAME, LUTZ.

WHAT'S THAT?

(Scratch) (Scratch) かかき

OKAY. I HAVE ENOUGH CLAY TAB-LETS NOW, SO HOW ABOUT YOU PRACTICE WRITING THIS?

...THIS IS MY NAME?

I LEARNED HOW TO SPELL EVERYONE'S NAMES WHEN LEARNING LETTERS.

THIS IS HOW YOU SPELL YOUR NAME.

YOU'LL NEED TO LEARN TO READ AND WRITE IF YOU WANT TO TRAVEL THE WORLD.

UH HUH.

ALL DONE!

YOU CAN'T REALLY CALL CLAY TABLETS A BOOK, REALLY.

BUT TO ME, THEY ARE, FOR THE FIRST TIME SINCE COMING TO THIS WORLD... I HAVE A BOOK.

I CAN READ BOOKS IN THIS WORLD TOO.

MAYBE... I'LL BE FINE HERE.

IN THIS WORLD WHERE BOOKS ARE TOO EXPENSIVE FOR COMMONERS TO BUY, I ENDED UP WITH A BODY SO WEAK, I CAUGHT FEVERS JUST FROM WALKING TOO FAST.

IT WAS SO BAD, I REALLY JUST... DIDN'T CARE IF I DIED.

I WASN'T ATTACHED TO A WORLD WITHOUT BOOKS.

I FEEL LIKE I'VE FOUND A REASON TO KEEP LIVING IN THIS WORLD.

...BUT.

NOW THAT I HAVE JUST A SINGLE BOOK, I HAVE SOMETHING PRECIOUS TO ME HERE.

ALL DONE, MYNE?

(Rustle)

WHAT'S WRITTEN ON THESE?

IT'S ALL THANKS TO EVERYONE'S HELP.

UH HUH.

...YES.

IT'S THE FIRST STORY I LEARNED.

THIS IS A STORY ABOUT THE STAR CHILDREN.

IT'S THE ONE MOM TOLD ME ON MY FIRST NIGHT HERE.

FIRST NIGHT?

MY FEVER WAS HIGH AND I COULDN'T SLEEP, SO MOM TOLD ME STORIES.

IT WAS BACK WHEN I FIRST BECAME MYNE.

YOU SEE, TUULI.

I WANT TO RECORD ALL THE STORIES MOM TELLS ME SO I NEVER FORGET THEM.

SO HER LOVE JUST HURT MY HEART AND MADE ME FEEL MORE ISOLATED.

AT THE TIME, I HADN'T ACCEPTED THAT I WAS MYNE NOW,

...BUT STILL.

WHEN I THOUGHT ABOUT MAKING A BOOK, THE STORY SHE TOLD ME THEN WAS THE FIRST THING THAT CAME TO MIND.

I SMILED A SINCERE SMILE.

BUT WON'T THE LETTERS JUST GO AWAY AGAIN?

THEY WILL, WHICH IS WHY I'M GOING TO BAKE THE TABLETS SO THEY DON'T.

THEN I CAN READ HER STORIES WHENEVER I WANT.

FOR MAYBE THE FIRST TIME SINCE I BEGAN LIVING HERE AS "MYNE"...

IT WOULD HAVE BEEN VERY MOVING IF THE STORY ENDED THERE, BUT...

(Boom!)

(Fizzle)

THE CLAY TABLETS CRUMBLED INTO SMOKING PIECES.

KYAH!

I TRIED BAKING THE CLAY TABLETS AS SOON AS I GOT HOME, AND THEY JUST EXPLODED.

LITERALLY, THEY EXPLODED.

MOM GOT REALLY MAD AT ME.

...WAIT. DOES THIS MEAN I'M BACK WHERE I STARTED?

(Shout)

OKAAAY...

CLEAN UP AFTER YOUR SELF!

(Shuffle)

SO I GUESS THIS IS MORE LIKE THREE STEPS FORWARD AND TWO STEPS BACK?

WELL, FINISHING THEM FOR A SECOND GAVE ME A BOOST OF MOTIVA-TION,

...WHAT SHOULD I TRY NEXT?

Ch.10: Finally the Forest End

HUH? WHERE'S MYNE...?

ザッ (Crunch)

ザッ (Crunch)

MORNING, RALPH! LUTZ!

MORNING, TUULI.

Extra Lutz and the Parue Tree

SHE'S WAITING AT THE GATE WITH DAD TODAY.

I'LL GET HER ON THE WAY BACK.

WAIT, DUH.

SHE'D GET A COLD IF SHE WENT TO THE FOREST IN THE WINTER.

ザッ (Crunch)

I'VE GOTTA GET A LOT FOR MYSELF TOO.

BYE!

TELL HER THAT WE WANT HER TO TEACH US MORE PARUE RECIPES, WOULD YOU?

OKAY, SURE.

ALRIGHT.

LUTZ, CLIMB UP ALREADY.

(Grasp)

ALRIGHT, SWITCH PLACES.

BE CAREFUL.

ガッ
(Grab)

ガッ
(Grab)

YOU CAN'T USE FIRE WHILE UP IN A TREE, AND NO BLADES CAN CUT THEM OFF.

TO GATHER PARUES, YOU HAVE TO USE YOUR BARE HANDS TO WARM AND SOFTEN THEM.

GOT IT.

HAAAH, SO COLD...

SHOULD JUST TAKE A LITTLE MORE.

...STILL, THANKS TO THE PARUE CAKES MYNE TAUGHT ME ABOUT, I'M MORE MO- TIVATED TO DO IT THAN I USED TO BE.

キ〆〆
(Squeeze)

NOT EVEN SWITCHING PLACES WITH MY BROTHER REGULARLY MADE THIS FEEL ANY BETTER,

ぐ ん っ
(Stretch)

AH!

AHHH!

シャラ
(Shake)

シャラ
(Shake)

ダッ
(Dash)

JUMP OFF!

WHA?!

LUTZ, THE SUN'S ALL THE WAY UP!

ボ ス ッ
(Slam)

NGH!

(Snap)

(Stretch)
シャラ

(Stretch)
シャラ

シュル
(Stretch)

シュル
(Stretch)

コブ゛
(Shake)

(Shrink)

...THEN VANISHES AFTER FLINGING OFF ALL ITS FRUIT.

A STRANGE TREE THAT GROWS UNDER SUNLIGHT...

I HOPE MYNE GETS TO SEE IT ONE DAY TOO.

A *FEYTREE* THAT ONLY APPEARS IN THE WINTER.

ASCENDANCE OF A BOOKWORM

OF A

BOOKWORM

I'll do anything to become a librarian!

Part 1 **If there aren't any books, I'll just have to make some! II**

AFTERWORD

Thank you for buying Volume Two of *Ascendance of a Bookworm's* manga adaptation! I'm Suzuka, the artist.

There were a lot more little things around Myne this volume. Hairpins, the baptism outfit, baskets, and so on. It was really fun to make lace hairpins and practice weaving with a machine at a real-life textile workshop.

In terms of book-making, she failed to make papyrus, and the clay tablets exploded. Please look forward to Myne's next idea.

New characters will appear next volume, so look forward to them. I am too. Finally, I'm sincerely looking forward to meeting you again in Volume Three.

-Suzuka

Special Thanks

AUTHOR: *Miya Kazuki*
CHARA DESIGN: *You Shiina*

Hattori Mio-san & Shimesaba-san   *My bosses in Tinami and TO Books!*

The workers at the weaving workshop.

* I asked Aine-san to do the coloring for the cover art this time* Thanks!!!

Afterword

To both those who are new to *Bookworm* and those who read the web novel: Thank you very much for reading Volume Two of *Ascendance of a Bookworm.*

This volume was all about life in the winter. Did you enjoy seeing Myne fighting to live in a world entirely unlike her own?

Here's a funny story. As Suzuka-sama sent me rough sketches and storyboards for this volume, she also sent me emails about how she did the things Myne was doing in real life: "I tried weaving cloth to improve my art," "Is this how Myne weaved the baskets?", "I made my own hairpin with lace flowers," and so on. I was really surprised to see the artist go that far. She used her experience to show in detail the process of making Tuuli's hairpin in an understandable way. Suzuka-sama, you're amazing! Don't you agree, reader? I mean, I even apologized when sending the rough plot outline to her since I knew drawing all the baskets and such would be a pain for her. (Ahaha.)

Still, it's a lot easier to understand what's going on with art to back things up. I was always worried about whether my readers would be able to picture how dark her home felt with only the candles and hearth for light, how there were a bunch of things placed into their small rooms for lack of space, how difficult and precise it is to hand-weave papyrus, and so on. But manga doesn't need detailed explanations where art will suffice. You can understand everything at a glance.

Though in return, where in the novel it was simple to just write "things got gradually messed up" and leave it at that, in manga you have to draw every indivudual thread that's getting messed up. Comparing the manga to the web novel made me realize just how different it is to communicate through text and art. Maybe you can have fun doing the same thing?

As you saw in this volume, Otto gave Myne a stone slate, and she's learning the alphabet bit by bit while working at the gate. She's having a successive string of failures and it looks like she won't even be able to beat Egyptian culture, but she's still running full speed towards her dream of making books. (While also tripping and falling at full speed.)

If you would like to, please enjoy your stay with the world of *Ascendance of a Bookworm*, drawn by Suzuka-sama.

Miya Kazuki

How to Actually Make Papyrus!

Shake Shake

Papyrus plant
(cyperus papyrus)

- contains sugar and oil in the stem
- Grows in tropical and subtropical regions

① cut the stem and peel the outer layer

② slice the stem into thin strips

③ put in water so bacteria will grow (this removes the sugar)

④ Line them up on cloth, overlapping sets of strips

⑤ squash them with pressure (this makes the strands connect together)

⑥ Let it dry

Polish the surface with shells or smooth stones

◇ALL DONE!

I DIDN'T REMEMBER ALL THOSE DETAILS!

NoOo!...

ASCENDANCE OF A BOOKWORM (MANGA) VOLUME 2
by Miya Kazuki (story) and Suzuka (artwork)
Original character designs by You Shiina

Translated by Carter "Quof" Collins
Edited by Aimee Zink
Lettered by Meiru

First published in Japan in 2016e gu by TO Books, Tokyo.
Publication rights for this English edition arranged through TO Books, Tokyo.

Find more books like this one at www.j-novel.club!

President and Publisher: Samuel Pinansky
Managing Editor (Manga): J. Collis
Managing Translator: Kristi Fernandez
QA Manager: Hannah N. Carter
Marketing Manager: Stephanie Hii

ISBN: 978-1-7183-7251-1
Printed in Korea
First Printing: November 2020
10 9 8 7 6 5 4 3 2 1

ASCENDANCE
OF A
BOOKWORM
I'll do anything to
become a librarian!
Part 2 Apprentice Shrine
Maiden Vol. 3
Author: Miya Kazuki
Illustrator: You Shiina

NOVEL:
PART 2 VOL. 3
ON SALE NOW!

Manga: **Hibiki Kokonoe**
Character Design: **Sukima**

I SHALL SURVIVE USING P⚫TIONS!

2

MANGA VOLUME 2
ON SALE
JANUARY 2021!

J-Novel Club Lineup

Ebook Releases Series List

A Lily Blooms in Another World
A Wild Last Boss Appeared!
Altina the Sword Princess
Amagi Brilliant Park
An Archdemon's Dilemma:
    How to Love Your Elf Bride
Arifureta Zero
Arifureta: From Commonplace
    to World's Strongest
Ascendance of a Bookworm
Beatless
Bibliophile Princess
Black Summoner
By the Grace of the Gods
Campfire Cooking in Another
    World with My Absurd Skill
Can Someone Please Explain
    What's Going On?!
Cooking with Wild Game
Crest of the Stars
Deathbound Duke's Daughter
Demon Lord, Retry!
Der Werwolf: The Annals of Veight
From Truant to Anime Screenwriter:
    My Path to "Anohana" and "The
    Anthem of the Heart"
Full Metal Panic!
Grimgar of Fantasy and Ash
Her Majesty's Swarm
Holmes of Kyoto
How a Realist Hero Rebuilt the
    Kingdom
How NOT to Summon a Demon
    Lord
I Refuse to Be Your Enemy!
I Saved Too Many Girls and Caused
    the Apocalypse
I Shall Survive Using Potions!
In Another World With My
    Smartphone
Infinite Dendrogram
Infinite Stratos
Invaders of the Roku
Isekai Rebuilding Pro
JK Haru is a Sex Wor
    World
Kobold King
Kokoro Connect
Last and First Idol
Lazy Dungeon Master
Mapping: The Trash-Tier Skill That
    Got Me Into a Top-Tier Party

Middle-Aged Businessman, Arise in
    Another World!
Mixed Bathing in Another
    Dimension
Monster Tamer
My Big Sister Lives in a Fantasy
    World
My Instant Death Ability is So
    Overpowered, No One in This
    Other World Stands a Chance
    Against Me!
My Next Life as a Villainess: All
    Routes Lead to Doom!
Otherside Picnic
Outbreak Company
Outer Ragna
Record of Wortenia War
Seirei Gensouki: Spirit Chronicles
Sexiled: My Sexist Party Leader
    Kicked Me Out, So I Teamed Up
    With a Mythical Sorceress!
Slayers
Sorcerous Stabber Orphen:
    The Wayward Journey
Tearmoon Empire
Teogonia
The Bloodline
The Combat Butler and Automaton
    Waitress
The Economics of Prophecy
The Epic Tale of the Reincarnated
    Prince Herscherik
The Extraordinary, the Ordinary,
    and SOAP!
The Greatest Magicmaster's
    Retirement Plan
The Holy Knight's Dark Road
The Magic in this Other World is
    Too Far Behind!
The Master of Ragnarok & Blesser

The White Cat's Revenge as
    Plotted from the Demon King's
    Lap
The World's Least Interesting
    Master Swordsman
Welcome to Japan, Ms. Elf!
When the Clock Strikes Z
Wild Times with a Fake Fake
    Princess

Manga Series:

A Very Fairy Apartment
An Archdemon's Dilemma:
    How to Love Your Elf Bride
Animeta!
Ascendance of a Bookworm
Bibliophile Princess
Black Summoner
Campfire Cooking in Another
    World with My Absurd Skill
Cooking with Wild Game
Demon Lord, Retry!
Discommunication
How a Realist Hero Rebuilt the
    Kingdom
I Love Yuri and I Got Bodyswapped
    with a Fujoshi!
I Shall Survive Using Potions!
Infinite Dendrogram
Mapping: The Trash-Tier Skill That
    Got Me Into a Top-Tier Party
Marginal Operation
Record of Wortenia War
Seirei Gensouki: Spirit Chronicles
Sorcerous Stabber Orphen:
    The Reckless Journey
Sorcerous Stabber Orphen:
    The Youthful Journey
Sweet Reincarnation
The Faraway Paladin
    gic in this Other World is
    ar Behind!
    ster of Ragnarok & Blesser
    herjar
    s of Marielle Clarac
    vanted Undead Adventurer

After Stopping a Truck with His
Bare Hands!!

Keep an eye out at j-novel.club
for further new title
announcements!